The Mystery
STUDY GUIDE

By
Dwayne Norman

Empyrion Publishing
Broken Arrow OK

The Mystery Study Guide
ISBN: 978-1484879696
Copyright 2013 by Dwayne Norman

Empyrion Press
Broken Arrow Ok
university@rickmanis.com

Unless otherwise indicated, all Scripture quotations are taken from the New King James Version of the Bible.

Contents

Chapter 1

The Power of the Gospel

In the book, *The Mystery,* read chapter 1, then read in your Bible the Scriptures designated below and answer the questions that follow. When you finish, check your answers in the answer key provided at the end of this book.

As you study these Scriptures and meditate on these verses, trust the Holy Spirit (our Teacher) to open up the eyes of your understanding and to give you the spirit of seeing and knowing into the eternal purpose that God accomplished for us in Christ through all of His sufferings, sacrifice and all that He did for us from the cross to the throne. The more real this becomes to you, the more you will be conformed to the image of Christ, and the more you will be transformed from glory to glory!

1. Read Matthew 22:29

    a. What will help us not to err or be deceived? _____

    _____

2. Who were the 2 most important men in all of history? _____

    _____

3. Read Romans 1:13-17

    a. What was Paul not ashamed of? _____

    _____

    b. What are Christians to live by? _____

4. Read Hebrews 11:6

   a. What do we have to have to please God? _____

      _____

5. Read I Corinthians 1:17,18; Romans 1:16

   a. What did Christ commission Paul to do? _____

      _____

   b. What is synonymous with preaching the Gospel? _____

      _____

   c. Where is the power of God? _____

      _____

   d. What are some of the meanings of "sozo" the Greek word for salvation?

      _____

      _____

6. Read I Corinthians 1:23;2:2

   a. What did Paul preach? _____

      _____

7. Read I Corinthians 15:1-4

   a. In its totality, the Gospel is all of God's Word, but what is God's definition of the Gospel in a "nutshell"?

   _____

   _____

Chapter 2

The Gospel of Calvary's Cross

In the book, The Mystery, read chapter 2, then read in your Bible the Scriptures designated below and answer the questions that follow. When you finish, check your answers in the answer key provided at the end of this book.

As you study the Word in this chapter, you are going to learn more about what the Gospel is and why we are to study and preach it. Also, you will better understand where the power of God is and how to release it into every situation.

1. Read Galatians 1:11,12

   a. What did Paul receive from Jesus? _____

   _____

2. Read Acts 8:5-8

   a. When Philip preached Christ (the cross, the Gospel) in Samaria, the lost got saved (which is the greatest miracle of all) and what other miracles took place?

   _____

   _____

   _____

b. What was released to work all of these *different* miracles when Philip preached the Gospel?

_____

I Corinthians 1:18 in the Amplified Bible says, "for the story and message of the cross is sheer absurdity and folly to those who are perishing and on their way to perdition, but to us who are being saved it is the **[manifestation of] the power of God.**

Therefore, whenever you and I preach the Gospel of the Lord Jesus, the power of God will be automatically manifested (to produce the new birth, healing, miracles, deliverance and whatever is needed) for the listeners if they only believe the message; because it's faith that activates the power that is *inherent* in the Gospel!

3. Read I Corinthians 15:1-4 again

   a. The Gospel message is for the lost and who else? _____

The lost only need to hear the facts (Jesus died, was buried and arose from the dead) to be saved, but as Christians, we need to <u>understand</u> the facts to grow up spiritually.

4. Read I Corinthians 3:10,11

   a. Who is our foundation? _____

   b. Healing, deliverance, miracles and all of the blessings of Heaven are by-products of what?

_____

c. In God's Kingdom, all "spiritual flights" are laid over at where?

_____

Chapter 3

The Identification Principle

1. Read Mark 4:14-20

   a. What does the devil want to steal out of our hearts? _____

   b. What does it mean to take a layover at Calvary? _____

   _____

   _____

2. Read Numbers 21:4-9

   a. What did the children of Israel have to look at to be healed? _____

   _____

   b. What they looked at was symbolic for what? _____

   _____

   c. Name some of the benefits or by-products of the death, burial and

   resurrection of Jesus? _____

   _____

3. Read Matthew 6:33

   a. What do we seek first? _____

b. Then what will the Lord do for us?_____

Like the Apostle Paul, in Galatians 1:11,12, we need a revelation of what God *finished* for us in Christ. A revelation comes when God speaks His Word into our hearts (which is referred to as a *rhema* word). It's like a light coming on inside of us, in our inner (reborn) man, then we have under-standing in what to say and what to do, and the result will be fruit for the Kingdom of God.

4. Write out the definition of the word, identify _____

_____

5. Read Galatians 3:13

a. Why could we be identified with Jesus? _____

_____

6. Read I John 4:17b

a. As Christians, how does God see us now? _____

_____

Remember, what those events at Calvary did for Jesus, they did the very same thing for you and me!

Chapter 4

The Identification Principle (Part 2)

1. Does spiritual death mean to cease to exist? _____

2. What is spiritual death? _____

3. Read II Corinthians 5:21

    a. There was a great exchange at Calvary. The Lord Jesus took our

    _____ and He gave us His _____

    b. Why did Jesus say, "My God, my God why have you forsaken

    me?" _____

    c. Did Jesus have to totally identify with us so that we could be

    totally identified with Him? _____

4. Read I Corinthians 15:21,22

    a. What came upon all of humanity because of Adam? _____

    b. What came upon all of humanity because of Jesus? _____

    d. Why were Adam and Jesus the 2 most important men in all of

    history?_____

    _____

5. What kind of men were Adam and Jesus? _____

_____

6. Write out the definition of the word, representation. _____

_____

7. Read I Corinthians 15:22

   a. What 2 terms (or phrases) in this verse describe representation?

   _____

8. Read Genesis 2:17

   a. How did Adam die the day that he ate of the fruit, since he did not

   die physically? _____

9. Read Hebrews 2:9

   a. What kind of death, besides physical death, did Jesus taste or

   partake of for every person? _____

10. Read Romans 5:12-19

   a. What kind of words are the words, all, one and many? _____

   _____

Chapter 5

It's All Yours in Christ

According to Romans 5:15, what God did for humanity *in Christ* was far greater than what the devil did to humanity *in Adam;* therefore, our future is bright and we can expect to experience every good thing that is ours *in Christ Jesus* our Lord and Redeemer!

1. Name some of the results or consequences that came upon the human race because of Adam's sin. _____

_____

2. When you hear on the news of the atrocities that people commit against each other, it reminds us that fallen man is still in_____.

3. Read Acts 14:6-15

   a. What 2 Christians were mistaken for gods? _____

   _____

   b. God wants to use His people to show the world that they are in

   _____, because they obey His commandments and walk in

   faith and love.

4. Read Romans 5:15,20

    a. Shouldn't it be *easier* to receive what God did for us in Christ than

    what the devil did for (against) us in Adam? _____

5. We need to operate in _____ to receive the manifestation of what
    the Lord *has already* done for us at Calvary.

6. Read Mark 11:23 & Philemon 6

    a. Our faith becomes effective or energized when we acknowledge or

    declare_____

    _____

Chapter 6

The First Adam and the Last Adam

1. Read Hebrews 4:6,10

   a. Because of the finished work of Christ, we can now enter into

      God's_____.

   b. What can stop you from entering into the rest of God? _____

2. Read Mark 11:23,24; II Corinthians 5:17

   a. Your faith is what you believe (in your heart), not what you feel

      and see; therefore, how do you walk? _____

3. Read I Corinthians 15:45,47

   a. Who is the last Adam? _____

   b. Why is He called the last Adam and not the second Adam? _____

      _____

      _____

    Our redemption is *complete* in Christ! Every area of our lives has been redeemed because Jesus was our substitute in every area. He *completely* identified Himself with us so that we could be *completely* identified with Him.

4. The reason that people can be born-again today is because Jesus was first _____ for us. He was the first fruits (I Corinthians 15:20).

5. Read Hebrews 7:1-10

   a. God gave the tribe of Levi full credit for paying tithes to Melchizedek when Abraham paid tithes to him; even thought Levi wasn't even born yet; because Levi was in _____.

   b. Did God identify (to consider and treat as the same) Levi with Abraham? _____.

   c. Is time a factor (important) when dealing with representative men? _____.

6. Read Romans 3:23; 5:12

   a. Spiritual death came upon the entire human race almost 6000 years ago because we all were in _____.

   When witnessing to the lost, they sometimes will ask me, "Why does God hold me responsible for what 1 man did almost 6000 years ago when I was not physically there?" Adam could have lived 10,000,000 years ago and what came on him would have come on us because he *represented* us.

7. If my 100th great grandfather had *physically* died when he was 7 years old, then I would have *physically* _____ in him when he was 7 years old. I would have <u>never</u> *physically* been born.

Chapter 7

Seven Identifications With Christ

1. If I did not like the physical characteristics that I got from my earthly father, would they disappear out of my life if I killed my father? _____.

2. Why? _____.

3. The phrases, "in Him, with Him, with us, for us" are representative phrases. These phrases always remind us that there can be no identification without _____.

4. What Scriptures tell us that Jesus was our *substitute* and took the curse *for us* so that we could be *identified with Him* in the blessing of Abraham coming upon us? _____

5. What did man need to be free from what the devil brought upon us through Adam's sin? _____.

6. Jesus ultimately came to save all of humanity, but what did He first have to do before He could make us into a new creation in Him? _____.

7. Does spiritual death reside in the inner or outer man? _____

Because of the nature (Adamic nature) of sin and death that came into Man, depression came into his mind, sickness and disease came into his body, poverty came into his finances and his entire being was affected.

8. Read II Peter 1:4

    a. As Christians, whose nature do we have in us? _____

9. Read Romans 6:1-11; Ephesians 2:4-6

    Write out the 7 areas of our redemption in our identification with

    Christ from the cross to the throne _____

    _____

    _____

    _____

10. To be firmly grounded in the love of God, we must be established in

    our _____

Chapter 8

Some Important Facts About Your Redemption

1. Read II Corinthians 5:14

    a. This verse does not say that if one died for all, then all were kept

    from dying. But is says that if one (Jesus) died for all, then all

    (humanity) _____.

    b. We could not kill the nature of sin in our spirits, so Jesus killed it

    for us through His _____.

2. Read I Corinthians 9:27; Romans 8:13

    a. Did Jesus' death and resurrection eliminate our flesh and its nature?

    _____.

3. Read II Corinthians 5:17,18: I Thessalonians 5:23: Romans 12:2

    a. Remember, man is spirit, soul (mind) and body. What part of man

    is a new creation? _____

    b. In a believer's newly recreated spirit, how many things have been

    made new? _____

c. What part of man needs to be renewed to God's Word?

_____

Having our minds renewed to these Truths from God's Word is of vital importance! The reason many Christians don't live and act like they are new creations is because they still don't have the reality in them that Christ took them out of Adam. The old man (old nature-sin and death) is dead! That sin nature (the old man) still exist in the world around us but it has been removed out of our spirits!!

4. Read Romans 6:11

   a. What do we need to reckon or consider, to be so in our lives?

   _____

5. Read John 15:1-4

   a. What does the word "abide" mean? _____

   _____

   b. All of our life and power comes from Jesus. He is the Vine and we

   are the _____

6. Read John 12:31-33

   a. What did the phrase, "to be lifted up" mean? _____

   b. Because Jesus was a representative man, the people did not realize

   that when they crucified Jesus, they crucified _____

7. Read Galatians 2:20

    a. Isn't true that when Jesus was nailed to the cross we were not at the mall or somewhere else; in the spirit, almost 2000 years ago, we were right there in Christ nailed to that cross? _____

8. Look at Romans 3:25,26

    a. Write out the definition for the word "propitiation" _____

    _____

Some Important Facts About Your Redemption

Chapter 9

More Important Facts About Your Redemption

1. Jesus was our propitiation or mercy seat. We could not go to the cross

   by ourselves so Jesus represented us and went to the cross as our

   _____

2. Read Luke 4:17-21

   a. Like Jesus did, where do we need to find ourselves? _____

3. Read Colossians 2:6-10

   What can be a physical result of sin in a person's spirit?_____

   _____

4. Is sin spiritual or physical? _____

5. Read Ephesians 2:1

   a. To be dead in sins and trespasses, is to be dead where? _____

   _____

Sin is disobedience to the commandments of God. If you use your body to do something wrong today and don't repent of it, you still need to be cleansed of that sin, but when your friends see you, they cannot see (with their physical eyes) your sin. Also, they cannot see (with their physical eyes) your righteousness in Christ because it's spiritual. They can see a demonstration in your actions of that sin or that righteousness.

6. Read II Corinthians 5:21; I Peter 2:24

   a. When Jesus became sin, He bore it *in* and not on His body;

   Therefore He bore it where? _____

7. Spiritual death does not mean to <u>cease to exist</u>, if it did, the devil, all

   demons, and all lost people would not exist. Jesus would have come

   to this earth and found no one to save. What does spiritual death

   mean?_____

8. Again, read II Corinthians 5:17,18

   a. As a Christian, the devil will try to bring back the "memory" of

   the old man and how he once acted, but it's <u>only</u> a memory.

   Therefore, how many natures do you have in your spirit? _____

9. Read Romans 6:11

   a. Did God give us full credit for all that Jesus did at Calvary? _____

10. Read Hebrews 2:14,15

a. The devil's power has been broken over us; so what avenue does

the devil have to use to get into our lives? _____

11. Read Romans 6:6-14

a. How are we (believers) in relation to sin? _____

The old man that sin had dominion over is dead; so he cannot be tempted anymore. A temptation would not be tempting to him since he's dead. Even though the devil can bring temptation against us, it has no power or dominion over us. We are dead to it, as far as sin is concerned, we **do not** have to yield to it anymore!!

More Important Facts About Your Redemption

Chapter 10

The Old Man is Dead

1. Write out the 5 important facts of our redemption _____

   _____

   _____

   _____

   _____

   _____

2. Who else did God see nailed to the cross when Jesus was crucified?

   _____

3. Read Colossians 3:8-12

   a. What do we need to <u>put on</u> now that we are born-again? _____

   _____

4. In the Gospels they saw (with their physical eyes) what happened to

   Jesus at Calvary, but in the _____, the Holy Sprit gives us

   a "behind the scenes look" at what Jesus did for us.

5. Read Hebrews 9:22

   a. There is no remission of sins without what? _____

6. Read Ezekiel 18:20; Hebrews 9:11-22

   a. The Lord Jesus had to shed His precious Blood through what? ____

   _____.

7. Read Hebrews 2:14 again

a. It was through _____ that Jesus destroyed him who had the
   power of death.

   The old testament animal sacrifices were types and shadows of what
Jesus did for us at Calvary, and they always died when they're blood was
shed. If Jesus only had to shed His Blood, then the Father did Him a
great injustice by having Him crucified, die and suffer all of the tortures
of hell.

8. Read I Corinthians 15:17

   a. The Apostle Paul said that we would still be dead in our sins if

   Christ is not _____.

   Therefore, Jesus had to die and arise from the dead.

I believe that *everything* that Jesus did and *everything* that He suffered for you and me can be summed up in 4 words, "the Blood of Jesus"! When we plead the Blood of Jesus, we are declaring all that Jesus did for the entire human race!

9. Read Galatians 2:20

    a. Your "self" is the real you: your spirit man inside your body

       (flesh). So, do we need to crucify our "self"? _____

    b. What do we need to crucify everyday? _____

The Old Man is Dead

Chapter 11

Did Jesus Die Spiritually? (Part 1)

1. What must you do to learn new doctrines and get new revelation from

   the Lord when you study the Bible? _____

   _____

2. Read Romans 5:14,17; 6:23

   a. What reigned over the human race because of Adam's sin? _____

      _____.

   b. According to Genesis 2:17, God told Adam that if he ate of the

      fruit of that tree, he would die that day; so, did he die physically or

      spiritually that day? _____

   The Bible says that 1000 years is as 1 day with the Lord (II Peter 3:8). That's true, with the Lord; but not with man. God would not tell me to wait 1 day, then go next door and witness to my neighbor, when He really means for me to wait 1000 years.

3. Physical death, sickness and poverty are all by-products of the nature

   or the law of sin and death. Therefore, how many times did Adam

   die? _____.

4. Read Isaiah 53:6

    a. What did the Father God lay on Jesus for all of us? _____

    b. Did He lay our sin on Jesus' knee, foot, arm, nose, stomach, mind

    or spirit? _____ .

5. Jesus <u>did not</u> commit sin. He was *sinless.* He took our sin upon

    Himself. Animals could not redeem us because we needed a

    _____ sacrifice. Animals don't have a spirit. They were

    not created in God's image; therefore, they could not fully identify

    with man.

6. Read Matthew 25:41

    Spiritual life is conscious existence and communion with God.

    What is spiritual death? _____

    _____

7. The word *everlasting*, in the Greek, means what? _____

    _____

8. Every human being will live or exist forever. But <u>they</u> can determine

    the geographical location of where that will be by whether they accept

    Jesus as their Savior or not (Romans 10:9). True or False? _____

Chapter 12

Did Jesus Die Spiritually? (Part 2)

1. Read Romans 6:23

    a. Many don't take sin seriously, but God does. If we sin, we need

    to repent, but what does it mean to repent?_____

    _____

    _____.

2. Remember, every human being is going to live forever. So, what

    does it mean for a Christian to have eternal life?_____

    _____

    _____.

3. Please write the definition of "identify" again._____

    _____

    _____.

4. Read Mathew 25: 31-46

    Hell and *everlasting* fire were prepared for the devil and the fallen

    angels, but who else did the Lord say would experience this horrible punishment?_____.

Some say that Jesus could not have died spiritually because God would cease to exist. We now know that spiritual death does not mean to cease to exist, but it means that you cease to exist in fellowship with God. Every person will exist forever; either with God in His Kingdom or with the devil in the lake of fire.

5. Read Ephesians 2:1

    a. How was man *dead* in his sins? Spiritually or physically?

    _____

6. Read Hebrews 2:9

    a. What did Jesus taste and experience for every person?_____

    _____

7. Read John 1: 1,2,14

    a. Jesus is the Word, the Word is God and the Word took on what?

    _____

Therefore, Jesus was all God and all man (spirit, soul and body). That, is the incarnation. He wasn't half God and half man. As a sinless man, He was able to sacrifice His spirit, soul and body for us; so when He bore spiritual death, He experienced (tasted) it in His spirit man. That is why He could experience separation from the Father God as our representative man.

8. Read II Corinthians 5:21

    a. What part of Jesus' spirit, soul and body did He bear sin in? _____

    _____

9. Read Isaiah 53:9 (King James translation)

    a. How did Jesus make His grave with the wicked since it was Joseph who actually made His physical grave? No one who dies physically can then go and bury himself. So, how did He make His grave?

    _____

    Note - some of our modern translations have changed the word "he" to the word "they" because they did not understand that Jesus bore spiritual death for us. In the margin of one very popular translation it says that the literal Hebrew should be translated "he", but they still translated it as "they"; admitting in their own translation that they were wrong.

10. Read Mathew 12:40; Ephesians 4:8-10
    a. Since Jesus made His grave with the *wicked* in the lower part of the earth, where did Jesus descend to after He died physically?

    _____

    _____

11. Read Isaiah 53:9 again
    a. In the margin of my Bible it says that the literal Hebrew for the

    word "death" should be translated in the plural "deaths". So, how

    many times did Jesus die? _____

In the Garden of Gethsemane, Jesus sweated drops of blood and asked the Father if there was another way. He knew He was about to suffer much more than Stephen suffered as the first martyr of the church. He knew that He was going to bear the sin of the entire human race and the result for Him would be a temporary separation from the Father; something He had never experienced in all of eternity past.

Chapter 13

Did Jesus Die Spiritually? (Part 3)

1. Jesus took our place and fully represented us, because there can be no

   identification without what? _____

2. Read Galatians 3:13,14
   a. According to verse 13, what did Jesus *become* for us when He

   went to the cross? _____

3. Read Leviticus 16:5-22
   a. How many goats did it take to fulfill this atonement every year?

   _____

   b. The high priest killed one goat, but where did they send the other

   goat?_____

   _____

   c. In the Hebrew, the phrase "not inhabited" means what? _____

   _____

   d. The second goat what a type of Christ who bore what for us? _____

   _____

4. Read Numbers 21:7-9; John 3:14
   a. What represented Christ that Moses put on a pole in the

   wilderness?_____

   b. What was brass a symbol of? _____

   c. What was the serpent a symbol of (remember Galatians 3:13)? __

   _____

Chapter 14

Did Jesus Die Spiritually? (Part 4)

1. Read John 3:14 again

   a. The Lord gave His own commentary of Numbers 21:8,9. Who was He referring to (symbolically) as the serpent on the pole? _____

   _____

2. Read I Timothy 3:16

   a. It says that Jesus was <u>justified</u> in the spirit. What does that mean?

   _____

   _____

   _____

   b. In the Greek, what does the word "justify" mean? _____

   _____

3. Read II Corinthians 5:21

   a. Since Jesus was made sin or unrighteous (again He did not commit

   sin. He was made to be sin for us); was it in His spirit-man or

   body?_____

The fact that Jesus had to be justified is another proof that He bore spiritual death in His spirit, by the very definition of justification. We could not be justified until the nature of sin and spiritual death was removed out of our spirits!

4. Read Isaiah 53:6 & Romans 6:23

    a. Where did God lay our sins on Jesus? _____

    b. What were the <u>wages</u> of our sin? What did it pay or produce in

       our lives? _____

    c. Therefore, for Jesus to pay the wages of our sin, He had to suffer

       what we suffered; because there can be no identification without

       what? _____

5. Read Philippians 2:5-8

    Even though Jesus was Deity, He emptied Himself of His Divine privileges. He became a man with a spirit, soul and body, so that He could identify Himself with us and experience our suffering. It was the Father who made Him to be made sin. And when Jesus became sin, the Father (in Heaven) did not become sin also. As a man, like you and me, Jesus could experience spiritual death without it affecting the Father.

6. Read Luke 23:46, Acts 14:23 & Matthew 12:40

    a. What does the word "commend" mean? _____

    _____

b. When the elders were commended to the Lord, did their spirits Leave their bodies and go to Heaven? _____

c. Where did Jesus say that He was going to go (after He physically died) for 3 days and 3 nights? _____

7. Read Ephesians 2:1,5 & I Peter 3:18

a. When Jesus came to the earth, how was the entire human race dead; spiritually or physically? _____

b. When we were made alive from being dead in sins, were we made alive spiritually or physically? _____

c. Since we were made alive **together** <u>with Christ</u>, then how must He have been made alive? Spiritually or physically? _____

There is no "togetherness" with Christ if we were not all made alive the same way!

8. Read Colossians 1:18 & Revelation 1:5

a. Jesus was the first born from the what? _____

Every mother calls their first born child, just their "first born"; not their first born from the dead. The first born from the dead identifies where Jesus was the first born from. He was the first man to be born-again. The only reason that we could pass from spiritual death to spiritual life is because He did. We got what He got! Praise The Lord!!

Chapter 15

Did Jesus Die Spiritually? (Part 5)

1. Look at Luke 23:43

In the Greek, this verse did not have a comma before or after the word "today". The King James translators decided where they thought it should go. The comma should be after the word "today". If I said, "I'm telling you today, you will be with me at the Mall" that doesn't mean that I'm going to the Mall today. It just means that "today" I'm letting you know that at some point I'm going to the Mall.

2. Read Ephesians 4:9,10 & Luke 16:19-31

   a. There were at least 2 compartments in Hell or Hades. Where did

   Lazarus go when he died? _____

   b. What part of Hell did the rich man go to when he died? _____

   _____

   c. According to Ephesians 4, what did Jesus do <u>before</u> He ascended?

   _____

   c. Since Jesus had to suffer what we were suppose to suffer, where

   did He descend to when He died physically? _____

   _____

3. Read Acts 2:22-24

a. Can a person who is physically dead suffer any physical pain? _____

b. After a lost person physically dies, what kind of pain will he suffer? Remember, the rich man in hell (Luke 16:24)

_____

4. Read Matthew 27:46

a. As horrible as the torture was by man on the earth and by the devil in hell; what was the worst thing that Jesus suffered? _____

_____

5. Read Hebrews 1:5,6 & Acts 13:28-33

a. Did Jesus become the Son of God when He was born of the virgin Mary? _____

b. Jesus is eternal. He always was, is and will be God's Son; so what did God mean when He said, "this day I have begotten you?"

_____

c. What <u>day</u> was Jesus born-again or begotten of God? _____

_____

Chapter 16

Made Alive With Christ

1. Read Ephesians 2:1,4,5

   a. Again, I want you to write out the definition of the word

      "identify"?_____

      _____

   b. Write out the definition of spiritual death. And remember, it does

      not mean to cease to exist. _____

      _____

   c. Why did Jesus have to be made alive from spiritual death to

      spiritual life? _____

      _____

   d. The phrases "In Christ, in Him and with Him" show togetherness.
      they remind us that there can be <u>no</u> identification without?

      _____

   The only way for God to accomplish in our lives what He so wanted
to do, was for Him to bring it to pass in the death and resurrection of
Jesus; so that He could give us full credit for it. Jesus did for us what we
needed to do, but couldn't do. In God's mind, He saw you and me (in
Christ) do everything that Jesus did! We truly are **Victorious**!!

2. Read Acts 5:20 & Romans 8:2

    a. What set us free from the nature or law of sin and death? _____

    _____

    b. When Jesus got eternal life. We got? _____

    Zoe is the Greek word for eternal life. It's the very life and nature of God. He wants everyone to have it, but the only way to experience what God has already done for us in Christ is to accept Jesus as our personal Lord and Savior.

3. Read II Peter 1:3,4

    a. Based on these Scriptures we've been studying, what is the nature

      of God? _____

    b. According to the definition of the Greek word "Zoe", the word

      "eternal" draws attention to what? _____

    _____

4. John 10:10

    a. What did Jesus come to give us? _____

    Having God's life (nature) within us, means more than just going to Heaven. Healing, deliverance, prosperity, joy, peace, wisdom and all of the blessings of Heaven are ours **NOW** through God's nature (the law of the Sprit of life in Christ) in our spirits!!

Chapter 17

Conquering and Raised With Him

1. Look at Colossians 2:15

    a. Every time you read in the Gospels about Jesus crucifixion, death,

    burial and resurrection, there will be a parallel Scripture in the

    _____ saying that we did the same things in Him!

    In the Greek, the word "spoiled" means to divest wholly of oneself, to
    put off. Satan and all his demons were (you could say) on Jesus trying to
    keep Him in hell, but when the life of God came into His spirit it was
    over! He put them all off! He rendered them powerless! And crushed
    their heads under the heals of His feet!!

    b. When Jesus conquered the devil, we _____ the devil!

    His conquest over sin, death, sickness, poverty and all of the curse

    was our _____!

2. Read I Corinthians 15:17

    a. On the cross, what did Jesus mean when He said, "it is finished"?

    _____

    _____

b. Did Jesus have to do any more than just die on the cross? _____

c. According to the Bible, our faith would be in vain or worthless if

Jesus did not _____ from the dead.

3. Read again Hebrews 2:14

a. Through Jesus _____ He destroyed him that had the power of
death.

b. Write out the Greek definition for the word "destroyed". _____

c. If a check has the word "void" stamped on it, can you cash it? _____

d. Is there any amount you could write the check for and be able to

cash it? _____

4. Read Ephesians 2:6 & Colossians 3:1

The resurrection of Christ is proof of His conquest over the devil and
all of hell. It's proof that Jesus did pay our penalty for sin and redeem us
back to God!

a. When someone has been raised from the dead it shows that

_____ has been overcome.

b. God wants all Christians to walk in _____

Jesus resurrection was 2 fold: spiritual and physical. Ours was the same. We just can't enjoy our immortal bodies until Jesus comes back for us, but we still got them when we were resurrected with Christ.

5. Read Colossians 3:1-14

   a. Because we have been raised together with Christ, we can set our minds on the things above. We can put off the old man and put on the new man. Write out at least 10 things that we can put off and at least 8 things that we can put on.

_____

_____

_____

_____

_____

_____

_____

_____

_____

_____

Chapter 18

Seated With Christ

1. Look again at Ephesians 2:1-6

   a. Write out the last 3 areas of our identification with Christ covered in verses 5 & 6 _____

   _____

   _____

   b. When are we seated together in the Heavenly places in Christ? ____

   _____

   b. What did Jesus do when He ascended into Heaven at the Father's right hand? _____

   c. The high priest in the old covenant never sat down because their work was never finished. The Lord Jesus sat down because he finished everything for us! When He sat down, we _____ down!

    d. After God created the worlds in the beginning, He rested on the 7th day. He did not rest because He was tired. He rested because He was finished. We are now at _____ in Christ!

    f. Hebrews 4:9,10 tells us that we have ceased from our own? _____

2. Read Ephesians 1:15-23

    a. We need to have a revelation or reality of how great God's power is inside of us. According to verses 19-21, it's the same power in us NOW that God used when He did what? _____

_____

_____

_____

    b. Just because everything is finished in Christ, doesn't mean that we automatically experience it. According to Hebrews 4:3, what do we have to do to enter or experience <u>our</u> rest? _____

Our faith in God activates this awesome power within us to bring to pass in our lives what the Lord Jesus accomplished or finished for us at Calvary.

3. Read Romans 10:17, Proverbs 4:20-22 & Joshua 1:8

    a. How does faith come? _____

b. What do we need to do day and night or on a regularly basis? _____

_____

4. Read Luke 10:19, Matthew 28:18-20, Romans 5:17 & Ephesians 1:20-23

   a. Because we are in Christ, what do we get to do that kings do? _____

   _____

   b. Name some of the things that we are ruling and reigning over? _____

   _____

   _____

   _____

Always remember, we get to live and operate down here, every day, from our place or position in Christ at God the Father's right hand in Heaven! All of the authority, power and dominion that goes with that position (seated at the highest place there is) is ours NOW to operate in on the earth! Your position is just as real and powerful even though you are not "physically" seated there! The president can operate in the same authority and power when he is "physically" in Florida, just as much as he can when he is "physically" seated in his chair in the oval office. Our geographical location may change but our place in Christ will never change!!

Chapter 19

In Him Through Covenant Loyalty

1. Read John 17:20,21; 15:5

   a. What does the phrase "in Him" describe? _____

   _____

   b. Who is the vine? _____. Who are the branches? _____

   _____

   c. Where does all life come from for the branches to bear fruit? _____

   _____

   d. Therefore, the phrase _____ is the hinge pin for our understanding the entire New Testament, and our being fruitful in God's Kingdom.

   e. The phrases "in Him, in Christ, together with Christ, with Christ"

   are all _____ phrases.

2. Read II Kings 24:11-20; II Chronicles 36:10-13; Ezekiel 17:11-21

   a. What did Nebuchadnezzar do to Zedekiah when he took over

   Jerusalem? _____

   _____

b. What do we mean when we say that God imposed a covenant upon

us? _____

_____

_____

3. According to Romans 8:17 & Ephesians 1:3

a. What did we get from God's covenant of love, mercy and grace?

_____

_____

4. Write out the definition of the word "covenant" from our text book.

_____

_____

_____

5. When 2 groups of people enter into a blood covenant, what would be

the first thing that they would get? _____

6. Read Genesis chapter 15

a. Abraham represented humanity and God represented Himself and

they cut or made a covenant, and it was an oath unto _____

b. According to Proverbs 18:24, who is the friend that sticks closer than a brother? _____

c. What happens if either party of a blood covenant don't keep their part? _____

d. After the blood covenant was cut between the 2 peoples, what was the last thing that they did together? _____

_____

e. What is an example of a blood covenant between a man and a woman? _____

7. In Psalm 63:3, as well as other references, the phrase "loving kindness" describes God's what? _____

Chapter 20

In Him

1. Read I Samuel 20, especially verse 16

    a. Who did Jonathan make a covenant with? _____

    b. What was the "common denominator" that brought David and

    Jonathan together? _____

David and Jonathan loved each other, but it was <u>not</u> a sexual love! They loved and served God, first and foremost, and when you truly love God you will obey His commandments. Please familiarize yourself with these verses, John 14:15,21; Leviticus 18:22; Romans 1:24-32; I Corinthians 6:9,10; Revelation 21:8

    c. Again, who is closer to you than your natural brother? _____

    _____

2. Read II Samuel 4:1-4 & II Samuel Chapter 9

    a. Who did David want to show kindness to for Jonathan's sake? ____

    _____

    b. Why did David want to show him kindness? _____

    _____

    _____

c. Did this man earn or merit David's kindness? _____

Because of our Blood Covenant with God in Christ Jesus, we can now confidently stand on Romans 8:32! Therefore, as He is, so are we (in Him) in this world (I John 4:17)!!

In Him

1. Chapter 1

    1a. Learning and obeying God's Word

    2. Adam & Jesus

    3a. The Gospel of the Lord Jesus
     b. Faith

    4. Faith

    5a. Preach the Gospel
     b. Preaching the cross
     c. In the message of the cross
     d. Deliverance, preservation and salvation

    6a. The cross

    7a. Jesus died, was buried and arose from the dead

2. Chapter 2

    1a. The Gospel

    2a. The lost got saved, miracles, deliverance and healings
     b. The Power of God

    3a. Christians

    4a. Jesus
     b. The death and resurrection of Christ
     c. Calvary

3. Chapter 3

1a. The Word of God
   b. Spend time studying and meditating on what God did for us through Jesus' sufferings and all that He did for us from the cross to the throne.

2a. The serpent on the pole
   b. Jesus becoming the curse for us
   c. Eternal life, healing, deliverance, prosperity, joy, righteousness, wisdom, protection and peace

3a. God's kingdom and His righteousness
   b. Add all these things unto you

4.   To make identical, to consider and treat as the same

5a. Because He was *first* identified with us

6a. As He sees Jesus

4. Chapter 4

1. **NO**

2. Spiritual alienation or separation from God

3a. He took our <u>sins</u> and He gave us His <u>righteousness</u>
   b. Because He was spiritually separated from His Father
   c. **YES**

4a. Spiritual death
   b. Spiritual (eternal) life
   c. They were the only 2 men who represented **ALL** of humanity. The entire human race.

THE ANSWER GUIDE

5.   Representative men

6.   Someone who stands in for someone else to serve as an official delegate or agent.

7a. In Adam & In Christ

8a. He died spiritually

9a. Spiritual death

10a. Representative words, words that show identification with someone

5.   Chapter 5

1.   Spiritual death, sin, sickness, disease, poverty and lack

2.   Adam

3a. Paul & Barnabas
 b. Christ

4a. Yes

5.   Faith

6.   Every good thing in us in Christ

6.   Chapter 6

1a. Rest
 b. Unbelief or disobedience

2a. We walk by faith

3a. Jesus
  b. The last Adam means that there will be no more Adams. No one will have to come and represent the human race any more. What God did for us in Christ at Calvary was finished and completed for eternity!

  4. Born-again

5a. Abraham
  b. Yes
  c. No

6a. Adam

  7. Died

7. Chapter 7

  1. No

  2. Because I got what he got. I was identified with him

  3. Substitution

  4. Galatians 3:13,14

  5. Death

  6. He had to kill all of us. He had to kill our old man, the old nature

  7. In the inner man

8a. God's nature

9a. Crucifixion, Death, Burial, Quickening (made alive spiritually), Conquering, Resurrection & Ascension (seated)

10. Identification with Christ

8. Chapter 8

1a. Died
   b. Death

2a. No

3a. His spirit
   b. All things have been made New
   c. His mind

4a. That we are dead to sin and alive to God in Christ

5a. To live constantly in the presence of the Lord Jesus
   b. Branches

6a. Crucifixion and death
   b. Themselves

7. It's very True

8. Sacrifice, atonement, substitution, mercy seat & expiation

9. Chapter 9

1. Substitute or sacrifice

2. In the Word

3. Sickness in their bodies

4. Spiritual

5a. Spiritually or in your spirit

6a. In His spirit

7. It means that you exist physically, but in spiritual separation from God

8a. Just One

9a. **YES**

10a. Deception

11a. We are **DEAD** to sin!

10. Chapter 10

   1. Jesus was our substitute

      There can be no identification without substitution

      Jesus became in His spirit <u>all</u> that we were while in Adam

      God credited our account with <u>all</u> that Jesus did for us in His death, burial and resurrection

      As He is now, so are we in this world

   2. All of humanity

THE ANSWER GUIDE

3a. The new man

4. Epistles

5a. The shedding of blood

6a. Death

7a. Death

8a. Risen

9a. No
  b. Our flesh

11. Chapter 11

1. Believe everything you read

2a. Death
  b. He died spiritually

3. Twice

4a. Our iniquity or sin
  b. His spirit

5. Spiritual

6a. Conscious existence and separation from God

7. Eternal, perpetual and forever

8. TRUE

12. Chapter 12

   1a. To turn from your sin to God and don't go back to it.

   2. To have God's nature in you and to have a conscious existence eternally in God's presence

   3. To make identical. To consider and treat as the same

   4. The cursed or all non-Christians, non-believers

   5a. Spiritually

   6a. Spiritual as well as physical death

   7a. Flesh

   8a. His spirit

   9a. He made His spiritual grave, by allowing Himself to be separated from the Father

   10a. Hell or the place of torments

   11a. Twice

13. Chapter 13

   1. Substitution

   2a. The curse

   3a. Two
      b. Into the wilderness or an uninhabited land
      c. A place of separation or desolate place

    d. Spiritual death

    4a. A serpent or snake
     b. Judgment
     c. The Curse

14.   Chapter 14

    1a. Himself (Jesus)

    2a. He was made righteous in His spirit
     b. To render just, innocent, free and righteous

    3a. His spirit-man

    4a. On His spirit
     b. Spiritual death, as well as physical death, sickness & poverty
     c. Substitution

    6a. To deposit, entrust and commit to
     b. NO
     c. In the heart of the earth or Hell

    7a. Spiritually
     b. Spiritually
     c. Spiritually

    8a. The dead

15.   Chapter 15

    2a. Abraham's bosom or paradise
     b. The place of torments

c. He descended
d. Into the place of torments

3a. NO
b. Spiritual pain

4a. Spiritual death or separation from His Father

5a. NO
b. That was when God raised Him from spiritual death to spiritual life
c. When He was raised from the dead

16.   Chapter 16

1a. To make identical. To consider and treat as the same
b. Spiritually separated from God
c. So that we could
d. Substitution

2a. The law of the Spirit of life in Christ Jesus
b. Eternal life

3a. Life
b. To the quality of that life, not to its duration in a temporal Sense

4a. Life (abundantly)!

17.   Chapter 17

1a. Epistles
b. Triumphed, conquered, conquest

2a. The old covenant was finished. He fulfilled all of the law. our redemption had not been completed yet because He had not yet died or arose from the dead.
  b. YES
  c. Rise

3a. Death
  b. To make of no affect, to bring to naught and to make <u>void</u>
  c. NO
  d. NO

4a. Death
  b. Resurrection life

5a. We can put off: fornication, uncleanness, evil desire, anger, covetousness, wrath, malice, blasphemy, filthy language out of your mouth and lying.

We can put on: tender mercies, kindness, humility, meekness, longsuffering, forgiving one another, bearing with one another and love

18.   Chapter 18

  1a. Made alive, resurrected and seated
  b. Right now
  c. He sat down
  d. Sat
  e. Rest

2a. When He raised Jesus from the dead and therefore conquered the devil and all of hell!
  b. We have to believe or operate in faith

3a. By hearing God's Word

b. Meditate the Word of God

4a. We get to rule and reign
  b. We are ruling and reigning over the devil, sin, all sickness and disease, poverty, depression, fear, doubt and all of the curse

19.   Chapter 19

  1a. Relationship
   b. Jesus, Christians
   c. The vine
   d. In Him
   e. Covenant

  2a. He imposed a covenant upon him.
   b. God set up a Blood covenant for man. He set the rules, terms and conditions. He did not ask our opinion about it at all. God did it all for us in Christ and we could not change it. We did not have to participate in it, but it would have been very unwise not to. We got the greatest blessing!

  3a. We are heirs of God, joint heirs with Jesus and we are blessed with every spiritual blessing in the Heavenly places in Christ.

  4. It's a binding oath that 2 people make which binds them together. This sacred oath is sealed in their own blood.

  5. A representative man

  6a. Death
   b. A blood covenant partner
   c. That person must die
   d. In our spirits, we have been sealed by the Holy Spirit with

the circumcision of Christ. In the old covenant, they were sealed with a physical circumcision, but ours is spiritual. Our flesh has not been cut, but the nature of sin and death has been cut (removed) out of our spirits.
  e. They ate a meal
  f. Marriage

  7. Covenant loyalty

20.   Chapter 20

  1a. David
  b. Their love for and mutual commitment to God
  c. A blood covenant partner

  2a. Mephibosheth
  b. To honor his covenant with Jonathan
  c. NO

About the Author

Dwayne Norman is a 1978 graduate of Christ For The Nations Bible Institute in Dallas, Texas. He spent 3 years witnessing to prostitutes and pimps in the red light district of Dallas, and another 3 years ministering as a team leader in the Campus Challenge ministry of Norvel Hayes.

He and his wife Leia travel and teach Supernatural Evangelism and train believers in who they are in Christ and how to operate in their ministries.

Contact the author at:

Dwayne Norman Ministries
124 Evergreen Ct
Mt Sterling KY 40353

Phone: 859-351-6496
E-mail: dwayne7@att.net

Contact Dwayne to order his other books and products:

The Mystery DVD's (12 hours) $50.00
The Mystery (book) $12.00
The Mystery Study Guide $10.00
The Awesome Power in the Message of the Cross $10.00
Your Beginning with God $10.00

Made in the USA
Charleston, SC
22 February 2014